SPIRITUAL FULNESS

Stephen Kaung

ISBN: 978-1-942521-54-9

Available from:

Christian Testimony Ministry
4424 Huguenot Road
Richmond, Virginia 23235

www.christiantestimonyministry.com

Printed in USA

CONTENTS

PREFACE

The following ministry was given by Brother Stephen Kaung at the Northeast Christian Weekend Conference, in October 2005. The theme for the conference was *Spiritual Fulness.* The conference concluded with a question and answer period, which is included as the last chapter.

The spoken messages have been transcribed into this booklet with minimal editing done for clarity, while maintaining the spoken form.

WHAT IS SPIRITUAL FULNESS?

Ephesians 1:22-23—And has put all things under his feet [that is under the feet of our Lord Jesus], and gave him to be head over all things to the church, which is his body, the fulness of him who fills all in all.

Ephesians 3:19—And to know the love of the Christ which surpasses knowledge; that ye may be filled even to all the fulness of God.

Ephesians 4:13—Until we all arrive at the unity of the faith and of the knowledge of the Son of God, at the full-grown man, at the measure of the stature of the fulness of the Christ.

Colossians 1:19—For in him [that is in Christ] all the fulness of the Godhead was pleased to dwell.

Colossians 2:9-10—For in him [that is in Christ] dwells all the fulness of the Godhead bodily; and ye are complete in him.

Shall we pray:

Dear heavenly Father, we bow in worship, thanking Thee for Thy gracious love towards us. Who are we that in these last days Thou should give us this opportunity, gathering us together, setting us apart to wait upon Thee, to hear Thy voice, to do Thy will? Oh heavenly Father, we thank Thee for Thy love, but at the same time we tremble before Thee lest we allow this time to pass away without really hearing Thy voice nor obeying Thy will. Do not allow us to come and to go as usual. We pray that Thou will create within us a real hunger and thirst after Thyself. We thank Thee for Thy precious promise: "Blessed are those who hunger and thirst for righteousness for they shall be filled." So we come before Thee as empty vessels. If we are already full, Lord, pour it out that we may really be filled with that which is above and not with that which is below. Do have mercy upon us that we will not take Thy word lightly. Oh Lord, teach us how to tremble at Thy word lest we depart from Thy truth. So we wait upon Thee, Lord, together. May Thy Spirit move in our midst. Oh Lord, we confess unless Thy Spirit open Thy word to us we are blind, we are helpless. So Lord, we pray that the Spirit of wisdom and revelation be given to us this time, that we may really know Thee and come to appreciate Thy fulness. Oh Lord, our confidence is in Thee. We give Thee all the glory in the name of our Lord Jesus. Amen.

Thank God for gathering us together again this time. I believe you all realize that the theme of this conference is *Spiritual Fulness.* I do not know how it hits you when you hear about spiritual fulness. What is your reaction? Do you think it is too glorious to be true? Do you think it is beyond our reach? Do you think that you know it all, that you already have it? What is your reaction?

As I meditated upon this subject, the more I meditated the more I began to realize the vastness, the greatness, the richness, the glory of the fulness of God. And yet it humbles me. It makes me feel how little of His fulness I know. I confess that the more I think about it, the more I think I am not fit to speak on this subject. So I am not going to speak to you on spiritual fulness. I am not worthy. The more I think of His fulness, the more I feel how little I know. The only thing that comforts me is that it does create in me a longing for His fulness. That is all I have. I long to know His fulness. So I dare not preach to you. What I will do is share with you my own meditation. I hope that you will go along with me as I meditate upon this glorious theme: "Spiritual Fulness." I hope you will meditate together with me. Hopefully, the Lord will create within us a deeper longing, thirsting, seeking, and pursuing after His fulness because this is the will of God. This is the hope of our salvation, and I pray to the Lord that He will empty every one of us that no one will think he knows, think he already has fulness.

Remember the church in Laodicea. They were full. They said, "We are rich; we lack nothing; we know everything; there is nothing more to add." That is their own judgment. But the judgment of the Lord is: "You are blind, you are naked, you are miserable, you are poor." So my prayer is that as we gather together there will be a spirit of humility. If you feel full, ask the Lord to empty you because only that which is emptied can be filled. May the Lord help us.

I tremble before the Lord. We gather year after year, and the coming of the Lord is drawing nearer and nearer. Are we prepared? Are we ready for Him? Can we see Him with empty hand, empty heart? I believe it is the mercy of God to gather us again and give us another opportunity that we may really repent before the Lord and earnestly seek to be filled with His fulness, that when we shall see Him we will not be put to shame. This is my heart's desire.

When you think of spiritual fulness, immediately it draws you to the prison letters of the apostle Paul—the letter to the Ephesians, the letter to the Colossians, and the letter to the Philippians. In the letter to the Ephesians it mentions the word *fulness* three times. "The church, the body of Christ, is the fulness of Him who fills all in all." Now, is it true? In Ephesians 3:19, in the prayer of the apostle Paul, how he prayed that our inner man would be strengthened, that Christ may dwell in our hearts, that we may begin to apprehend with all the saints the love of Christ which is beyond understanding and be filled with the fulness of God. "Filled with the fulness of God"—how

7

glorious that is! And then you turn to chapter 4:13: "That we may one day all arrive at the unity of the faith and of the knowledge of the Son of God to the full-grown man, to the measure of the stature of the fulness of Christ." Think of that! "The fulness of Christ."

In Colossians 1:19 it says: "In Him [in Christ] all the fulness of the Godhead was pleased to dwell." Thank God for that. Then in Colossians 2:9-10: "In Him [in Christ] dwells all the fulness of the Godhead bodily; and ye are complete in Him." A promise! And aside from the word *fulness,* in these two letters you find other words like *full, fill, all, every, riches, glory, complete, perfect.* All these words give us the impression of fulness. So we believe that it is the will of God that He wants us to know His fulness, not to know it mentally but know it experientially.

Now for our meditation we would like to ask the question: What is spiritual fulness? Where can we find it? Is it available to us? And then, God willing, next time we will meditate on: How do we apprehend spiritual fulness? We do not want to know spiritual fulness just mentally. We want to apprehend that fulness personally and corporately to the glory of God. So this morning we would like to share together, to meditate together on: "What is Spiritual Fulness?" Do we know this fulness?

THE FULNESS OF SIN

The natural man does not know the things of God. The world does not know this spiritual fulness. The only fulness this world knows is the fulness of sin, the fulness of iniquity, the fulness of violence, and the fulness of rebellion. That is the fulness we know. It is all negative. We have no idea of that positive, spiritual fulness.

In Genesis 6, during the time of Noah, God looked upon this earth. As man increased in number, God said, "My Spirit will not strive anymore with man because he has become flesh." The world was full of violence and the wickedness of man. Even the imagination of the thoughts and hearts were evil continuously. God could not bear it anymore, and He said, "I have to judge." And you remember that in the flood only Noah and his family found grace before God. That is the fulness the world knows.

9

Again in Genesis 18 and 19 God came to Abraham and said, "I cannot hide anything from him because I know he fears me, and he will tell his latter generations about Me." And God shared with Abraham. The voice of Sodom and Gomorrah rose up to heaven. The evil of those cities was so full and God said, "I come down to investigate." And He came down to judge. Sodom and Gomorrah and the neighboring cities were burned with fire from above. That is the fulness the world knows.

In Genesis 15 God made a covenant with Abraham, and He promised to give him the land of Canaan. But God said, "There will be four hundred years that the children of Israel will be slaves before they can possess their possession because the iniquity of the Amorites is not yet full." How patient is our God! He will not judge before time. He will wait. His longsuffering is misunderstood, but He does not want anyone to perish but all to come to salvation. But one day, when the iniquity was full, judgment would not delay.

We are living in a time no better than the time of Noah. "As the time of Noah so shall be the coming of the Son of Man" (see Matthew 24:37). We are living in a time no better than Sodom and Gomorrah, maybe even worse. We are living in a time like the seven tribes of Canaan. Their sin, the voice of their wickedness rose to heaven, and heaven came down. We are living in a most perilous time, a most dangerous time. All we know is violence; all we know is killing; all we know is sin; rebellion is everywhere. Do you think that our iniquity is almost full? Do you think the longsuffering of God will come to an end? Do you think that judgment is coming to this world? This is the time we are living in. This is a day, I believe, of the fulness of sin, of iniquity. Can you think that mankind can degenerate so low as today? Things unthinkable, unimaginable are happening. Thank God for His longsuffering! But for how long? I believe the day is coming; judgment is at the door. We need to wake up and be ready, be prepared. As the Bible says, when people think of what is going to happen, they are frightened to death. But to us the word of God says, "Lift up your head because your redemption draws nigh." Thank God.

Thank God He loves us so much; He loves the world so much, He will not let us go. He gives us hope. He shows us there is a fulness which is positive and glorious. It is spiritual fulness, not earthly, not natural, not devilish. It is heavenly, spiritual, of God, and He wants us to know that fulness, even to enter into that fulness. Can you imagine that! But this is our blessed hope.

Where can you find spiritual fulness? It is not the fulness that we know on earth. I do not know how you feel. I am tired of this fulness of iniquity. We need the glad tidings, and thank God it is already here. If we are going to meditate on spiritual fulness we have to forget ourselves. In ourselves there is no fulness. The only fulness in you and me is fulness of sins, rebellion, iniquity, wickedness, and violence. May God deliver us from ourselves. We have to leave ourselves behind and go to the source of spiritual fulness.

THE SOURCE OF SPIRITUAL FULNESS

Where is the source of spiritual fulness? You cannot find it on earth. You cannot find it in mankind. You cannot find it in the world. You cannot find it in yourself. It is not there. What is there is just the opposite. So we have to return to the beginning: "In the beginning God...." God is the only source of spiritual fulness. He is full from the beginning to the end. There is no development in God. Nothing can be increased; nothing can be decreased. He is the same yesterday, today, and forever. He never changes. He is always full to the fullest. That is God.

When you think of the fulness of the Godhead, it is beyond us. Even the apostle Paul was lost in words. He said, "What length, what width, what depth, what height!"

The fulness of the Godhead is immeasurable, incom-prehensible; it cannot be fathomed; it cannot be described. Fulness.

His Love

Can we fully understand the fulness of His love? We know something of love, but the love is earthly; it is human, the best of man. Yet when you compare it with the love of God, it is *unlove*. Only God's love is absolute, wholly self-sacrificial, pouring out without reservation, love beyond measure.

13

His Righteousness

When you think of His righteousness, all our righteousness is as filthy rags. It cannot cover our nakedness. Just like Daniel cried out, "Because I see Your glory, my beauty turns into corruption." He fell down as dead. Are you so righteous, so self-righteous, thinking that you are the only one on this earth that can stand before the righteous Judge? You fool yourself. No one can come to the presence of God without being smitten to death. His righteousness is the only righteousness that is right, absolutely right, pure and holy. We have no righteousness of our own. We should repent in dust and ashes. That is the experience of Job, the righteous man in his world, perfect. How he held on to his self-righteousness, until he saw the glory of God. He said, "I abhor myself; I hate myself. I repent in dust and ashes." The righteousness of the Godhead is beyond our understanding.

His Holiness

Think of the holiness of God. Sometimes we sing, "Holy, holy, holy, Lord God Almighty." But how much do we understand God's holiness? He is so absolutely separated. He stands all by Himself. There is no one His like, no one His comparison. He is alone. He is different. On the Mount of Transfiguration Peter tried to put Moses and Elijah on an equal footing with our Lord Jesus. God intervened. God said, "No! There is only My beloved Son." God took Moses and Elijah away. They looked up seeing nobody but Jesus only. Holy.

Brothers and sisters, I question myself. How much do I know the holiness of God? I know almost nothing.

His Light

God is light. There is no darkness in Him; there is no turning nor shadow. He is light, eternal light, perfect light. How light are we? We think we walk in the light but when we compare with Him who dwells in the light, who is light, our light turns to darkness. We need to repent; we need the blood of our Lord Jesus to cleanse us. Even the tears of our repentance need to be cleansed with His precious blood.

His Mightiness

God is almighty. We cannot even measure His mightiness. How much do we apprehend His mightiness? We sing the hymn: "Mighty is His name"; but how much do we experience His mightiness?

We could go on and on and on because God is infinite. He has no limit; He is full all the time. Nothing can take away His fulness. That is God. We may have a little understanding of the fulness of the Godhead. We may have a glimpse of the glory of God, but we cannot comprehend His vastness, His greatness, His richness, His glory. It is beyond us.

The more l meditate on the fulness of God the more I confess I know nothing. I ask God for mercy. Oh, how I long to know Him! But when you meditate upon God, upon His fulness, you can almost say you see it from afar, dimly, but you cannot get to it. God is a mystery. He is there but so remote, so transcendent, far beyond our reach. We can think a little bit, but that is all. If that is the case, it condemns us instead of justifying us. The more you think about God, the more your conscience smites you. But thank God, He loves us. He wants to make His fulness available to us. It is not His desire to let us know a little bit of His fulness and be condemned. That is not the will of God. The will of God is that He might bless us, He might share His fulness with us. His love is such that He wants to share it with us; but how?

THE WORD BECAME FLESH

The Word became flesh and tabernacled among men, full of grace and truth. If God remains in heaven He is beyond us. We are condemned; we are finished. But thank God, He came into this world. "God so loved the world that He gave His only begotten Son." One day, in the fulness of time, God's Son came into this world. The Word, the full expression of God took up a human form and dwelt among men, full of grace and truth. Do we appreciate what God has done? This is the only hope to us. He who is incomprehensible, transcendent, beyond, remote, has humbled Himself.

Philippians says, "He who is equal with God, and that is not something to be grasped at." That is who He is, forever is, eternally is: equal with God, God Himself. But the Son, for the love of God, emptied Himself. He cannot empty Himself of His deity because that is what He is; He is forever God. But He emptied Himself of all the glory, the position, the power, the worship, the honor, and took upon Himself a bondman's form. He came to be a bondman of God. He came to show us what God is. He came to show us the fulness of the Godhead; not a little, not almost, but full. It pleases God to have His Godhead dwell in Him. In Him the fulness of the Godhead dwells bodily. In other words, in that body, incarnated body, Jesus, all the fulness of the Godhead dwells; nothing less, nothing more. In other words, the fulness of the Godhead has been brought into this earth, from heaven to earth, to make it visible, to make it understandable, to make it touchable.

THE APOSTLES FELLOWSHIP HIM

In I John 1:1 it says, "That which is from the beginning...." That refers to our Lord Jesus because He is the Word. He is with the Father from the beginning. "That which is from the beginning, that which we have heard." Where did we hear Him? We heard about Him from the prophets, from the Old Testament, that He was coming. "That which we have seen with our eyes." The apostle John said, "We have seen with our eyes." How true it is. They saw the incarnated God. They not only saw Him, they contemplated Him. They began to understand Him, that He is not just a man. He is altogether different; He is God. He is God and Man in one. He is a Man who demonstrates God to us, the fulness of God to us. We have contemplated that which we have touched because He rose again. He could be touched. He said to Thomas: "Put your finger into my side; put your finger into my hands and see the holes there." The bleeding hands, the bleeding side could be touched.

The apostles who fellowshipped with the Lord fellowship with us. They are written in the word. Today, we can fellowship with the One who was from the beginning and was prophesied by the prophets, the One who came into this world, died, rose again, is now in heaven, and is coming soon. Oh, thank God, that which is intangible, incomprehensible, beyond our understanding, our reach, has already come to us. The Bible says, "No one knows the Father but the Son who is in the bosom of the Father; He declares Him" (see John 1:18). The prophets declared God in a limited, small way, in pieces and bits, here a little, there a little, but in the last days the Son declared the Father in fulness. The Lord said, "If you see Me you see the Father"; nothing less, nothing more. It is all here.

FULL OF GRACE AND TRUTH

When our Lord was on earth, He was full of grace and truth. In other words, He brought the grace of God to mankind; He brought the truth of God to mankind. When you read the gospel of John, the whole book illustrates our Lord Jesus full of grace and truth during His days on earth.

When Nicodemus came to the Lord, he wanted to be taught that he may be able to do something more to qualify him for the kingdom of God. But our Lord Jesus told him the truth: "Verily, verily, I say unto you, unless you are born from above you cannot even see the kingdom of God" (see John 3:3). Verily, verily, truly, truly.

The Samaritan woman was full of sins, and our Lord Jesus said, "If you know who is talking to you, you will ask Him and He will give you water that will become a fountain within you overflowing forever. You will not be thirsty again" (see John 4:14). How gracious our Lord is!

The man at the pool of Bethesda was infirm for thirty-eight years, always hoping that one day he might be the first one to enter into the pool and be healed when the angel stirred the water. But somebody always got in before him. Hope against hope, hopeless. The Lord said, "Do you want to be healed?" (see John 5:7). How sweet that sounds! How gracious—words of truth, acts of grace.

We could go on and on. That is what He is. He brought the grace of God to mankind; He brought the truth to mankind. He is grace; He is truth. Outside of Him there is no grace. Aside from Him there is no truth. Every truth is in Him; every grace is from Him. This is our Lord. He has demonstrated to us the fulness of the Godhead. What mercy! What love! What grace! What truth!

21

But if our Lord Jesus should come into this world two thousand years ago, live for thirty-three years, showing us the truth and grace of God, save sinners, forgive sinners, and say, "I will not condemn you; sin no more. Go in peace," touch the untouchable, heal the sick, open the eyes of the blind, raise the dead, cast out the demons, and demonstrate to the world the spiritual fulness of God, what blessing, what benefit would come upon the world?

But sometimes do you have this kind of feeling? "Oh, if I had lived two thousand years ago, if I had lived during the time of Jesus, if I lived in Judea, if I had had the opportunity to see our Lord Jesus and be touched by Him and hear Him, how blessed I would be. But unfortunately I am two thousand years too late." Can it be true? It can be true. If our Lord Jesus had come into this world, done all these things, said all these truths, and then on the Mount of Transfiguration exited from the world, do you know what would have happened? Only those people who lived in the time of Jesus and who had the privilege of seeing Him, hearing Him, and being touched by Him, would have been blessed, but no more. The fulness of God would have come and returned to heaven, and it would still be beyond our reach.

Thank God, He did not exit from the world from the Mount of Transfiguration. He could have done that. Heaven would be ready to receive Him, but He refused. He had to come down, turn His face towards Jerusalem, towards Calvary, towards death. That is what He came for. He came to die, not just to live. If He did not die, we all die; He alone will live. But because He went to Calvary, on the cross He sealed our redemption. In other words, all that He said, all that He did while He was on the earth, He said and did on the basis of Calvary, of the cross.

How can He tell an adulterous woman, "I will not condemn you; go in peace"? It is true, nobody could condemn her. Our Lord challenged them and said, "If anyone has no sin, cast the first stone." And then our Lord bowed His head and wrote on the earth. In other words, He was ashamed to see these people who thought they were more righteous than this adulterous woman, but He knew they were just as sinful. So from the oldest to the youngest, and we who are the oldest had to exit first, they exited until there was nobody there. Nobody was fit to cast the stone except the Lord. He could do it; He should do it. He must do it according to the Law, but He said, "No, I will not condemn you." On what basis? It is the basis of Calvary's cross. He did not condemn her because He condemned Himself. He took the place of that adulterous woman. "I die for you, and because of that I can forgive you."

Remember what He did on Calvary's cross? "Father, forgive them for they know not what they do." How can He even ask the Father to forgive such hideous sin, crucifying the Son of God? On what basis can the righteous God forgive? It is because our Lord offered Himself as our substitute.

Everything He did on earth is on the basis of Calvary's cross. Every truth He said is sealed by the finished work of Calvary's cross. It is the cross that consolidates everything. In other words, the fulness of God that had been brought into this world was now being sealed for eternity. People who lived before Calvary's cross looked forward to that cross to be forgiven. People who live after Calvary's cross look backward to the cross and claim what the cross has sealed, confirmed eternally for us.

Oh, the love of God! We do not need to live two thousand years ago. We do not need to go back to Palestine in order to find Him. He is now in heaven and with us. Everything that He has done, everything that He has spoken is all available to us today. Thank God for that! I cannot thank God enough for Calvary. He said, "It is finished." All is done. Now, that which is intangible has become tangible. That which is remote has been brought nigh. That which is a mystery is now a revelation. So as I meditated upon it I bowed in worship. How good is our God!

ANOTHER COMFORTER

But then, even though Calvary's cross is eternal, and has made all that our Lord did and said on earth eternal truth, eternal grace, how did it come to me? The truth is there; the finished work is there; redemption is there; fulness is there, is on earth, and is no longer related by time. It is timeless; anyone can have it. But how can all the fulness of Christ become real to *me*? Thank God, He provides for that too.

Even before His death, our Lord Jesus said, "Do not be sorrowful; I go for your sake. If I do not go the other Comforter, another Comforter will not be able to come. I was in the flesh. I could be with you but not forever. But now if I go I will ask the Father to send you another Comforter, another One just like Me. The only difference is because I was in the flesh with you, I cannot be forever with you. But when the another Comforter comes, the Holy Spirit of truth, He is Spirit, He shall be in you. He will never leave you or forsake you, and He will teach you all things concerning Me. He will bring all things about Me to you and make Me real in your life."

This is the work of the Holy Spirit. Thank God, not only is there the finished work of Christ on Calvary's cross to make it eternal, available, finished, prepared, and open, but the Holy Spirit came to bring us into all truth. The Holy Spirit is the Spirit of grace. He brings Christ into us and us into Christ. In other words, it is by the Holy Spirit who dwells in us daily, hourly, moment by moment, without ceasing. He is there bringing all that is of Christ to us; that is, to bring the fulness of the Godhead to us. Therefore the Bible says, "In Him all the fulness of the Godhead dwells bodily, and ye are complete in Him." This is the secret. We thank God the Father, we thank God the Son, we thank God the Holy Spirit.

I would like to conclude by just reading one passage because I feel that is the only thing I can conclude with.

Romans 11:33-35: "O depth of riches both of the wisdom and knowledge of God! how unsearchable his judgments, and untraceable his ways! For who has known the mind of the Lord, or who has been his counsellor? Or who has first given to him, and it shall be rendered to him? For of him, and through him, and for him are all things: to him be glory for ever. Amen."

THE WAY TO SPIRITUAL FULNESS

Philippians 3:8—But surely I count also all things to be loss on account of the excellency of the knowledge of Christ Jesus my Lord, on account of whom I have suffered the loss of all, and count them to be filth, that I may gain Christ.

Let's have a word of prayer:

Dear Lord, as we continue in Thy presence we look to Thee to keep it in the spirit of worship, of focusing upon Thyself, of forgetting ourselves and letting the Spirit of the Lord lead the way to spiritual fulness. We confess, Lord, how easily our eyes turn away from Thee to look upon the world, look upon ourselves, look upon others, look upon environments, and we lose sight of Thee. Oh, dear Lord, keep us fixed on Thee. Do not allow us to drift, to falter, but we do desire to offer ourselves to Thee. And Thou are the only one who is able to keep us to the very end. Lord, Thou hast opened the heaven for us. May that heavenly light continue to shine upon us, and in that glorious light we see Thee and we worship Thee. We ask in Thy precious name. Amen.

The theme for this time is *Spiritual Fulness*. Again I want to tell you that I do not feel fit to teach you on spiritual fulness. I want to be with you, meditating together with you on this glorious subject, looking to the Spirit of God to lead us into the truth. That is my prayer.

We began by meditating on: What is spiritual fulness? Where can it be found? The very term *spiritual* fulness limits the meaning of fulness. In other words, it turns us right away from thinking of worldly fulness, earthly fulness, carnal fulness. We are thinking of that which is spiritual, that which is eternal, that which is heavenly, that which is divine. That is the fulness that we long for, and that is the fulness that our God has provided for us. And it is His will that we be filled with that fulness. You cannot find that fulness in the world. You cannot find that fulness even in religion.

The Corinthian believers were believers; they had the life of Christ in them. They had all the potential for spiritual fulness, and yet they turned their eyes away from the Lord and looked to the world. They tried to find that fulness in the world, but it is not there. What is there is strife, contention, party spirit, sin, love of self, disorder, and disbelief. And the apostle Paul had to remind them: "It is Jesus Christ and Him crucified."

The Colossian believers were believers. That is why we are talking about spiritual fulness among ourselves. How easily we who have already believed in the Lord Jesus, will be led astray, forgetting that spiritual fulness can only be found in the Lord Jesus and nowhere else. And yet the Colossian believers had such a good beginning. They had faith, they had love, they had hope, and yet they were enticed to shift their attention from Christ Jesus. They were deceived into thinking that Christ alone cannot make you full. You have to keep the law. You have to do something. You have to believe in philosophy, in the teaching of man. They were sincere. They tried to find fulness, but they were led astray. The apostle Paul had to correct them and say, "All the fulness of the Godhead dwells in Christ Jesus bodily, and you are complete in Him."

Unfortunately, even among God's people today, we try to find fulness in places other than our Lord Jesus, and the result is tragic. So let us remember that God is the source of fulness. It is out of His fulness He created all things. All things are to manifest the glory of God, but unfortunately, sin entered into this world and spoiled everything.

But thank God, He loved us so much He will not let us go; therefore He sent His only begotten Son into this world. The Word became flesh and tabernacled among men, full of grace and truth. God demonstrates His fulness in the Person of our Lord Jesus; nothing short of fulness. His grace is full; it cannot be increased. His truth is full, everlasting. That is what we find in the life of our Lord Jesus. He is the expression, the manifestation, the very substance of the fulness of God. Thank God, our Lord Jesus did not come just to demonstrate God's fulness—what grace is, what truth is, for if He had not gone to the cross, it would not be available to us today. Thank our Lord Jesus, He sealed that fulness of the Godhead by His death, and because of Calvary's cross all the fulness of the Godhead is now available to us. If we believe, if we obey, it is ours. And thank God, He gave us the Holy Spirit. He is the Spirit of truth, the Spirit of grace, and He lives in us to make everything that our Lord has done two thousand years ago our living experience.

SUBJECTIVE EXPERIENCE

Now we would like to go on and meditate on how we really apprehend personally and together this spiritual fulness. In other words, in our first meditation we dealt mostly with eternal truth. Our Lord Jesus said, "I am the truth." What is eternal truth? Eternal truth is something that God has done through our Lord Jesus, and whatever He has done on Calvary's cross is eternal. It never changes. It is always there, always ready, always available, always working. But how does truth become our personal experience?

So now we would like to get into experience. Truth is objective; that is to say, it is outside of us. It is there, available, but outside of us. Now we want to see how the truth of spiritual fulness can become our daily, living, real experience, so that we can apprehend the love of God with all the saints. Because we are dealing with this matter of spiritual experience, I feel that it is better for us to find an example, a role model for us in our meditation. Of course, our Lord Jesus is the perfect example, but probably we will say, "He is God, although He is also Man." Aside from our Lord Jesus, where can we find someone who has really experienced spiritual fulness to a greater degree? I will not say to the fullest degree, because none can say that, but someone who has experienced spiritual fulness to such a great degree that he may help us and show us how to get into spiritual fulness. So our meditation will be on "The Way to Spiritual Fulness."

PAUL'S LIVING KNOWLEDGE OF SPIRITUAL FULNESS

I think everybody who studies the Bible agrees that if we want to find a New Testament example it is Paul. Paul himself testifies that by revelation he knows the mystery of Christ, but what he shares with us shows that he has the living knowledge of the fulness of Christ. So we would like to use him as our example because he is human as we are.

First of all, we know this man Paul was originally called Saul. He was named after the first king of Israel. Saul means "asked for." He was a young man, very different from other young people. I would say he was a man seeking for fulness. He was wise enough not to try to seek fulness in the world. Many young people do not seem to have that wisdom. As young people we think we can find our fulness in the world. If we have the riches, the wealth, the fame, the position, all that the world can offer us, then our life will be full. Foolishness!

But this young man was different. Paul did not try to find fulness in his life from the world. He turned away from the world, even as a young man, which was most unusual. He tried to find fulness in religion, in Judaism. He tried to find his fulness in the Law, the Mosaic Law. He was dealing with shadow not with reality. Even though the Law came from God, yet the Law is only a shadow showing us the reality. But that young man Saul was so absorbed in the Law of

Moses. He was a disciple of Moses. He was such a fervent disciple he became a Pharisee. At no time in history would there be many Pharisees; probably the most will be two or three thousand.

He was not like the other Pharisees. He was a true Pharisee, a Pharisee of Pharisees, a Hebrew of Hebrews. He studied the Law diligently. He tried to keep every letter in the Law. He could even boast of himself: "According to the righteousness of the Law I am blameless." What a young man he was! He trusted in himself. He trusted in his own work. He trusted in his own righteousness. He was more advanced than his contemporaries. He was zealous for the tradition of the fathers to such an extent that he became the chief persecutor of the followers of Jesus Christ. Why? Because according to human, religious estimation the Lord Jesus was an impostor of Judaism. He should be crucified: "Away with Him!" Saul was so zealous. He was the chief persecutor of believers at his time. All the time he was seeking for fulness. He thought he was serving God, that he was doing God a great service, not knowing he was in darkness, blind, naked, miserable. He was sincere, but deadly, wrongly sincere. God looks upon the heart. God loved that young man. In spite of all that he did, God knew his heart. His heart longed for fulness, but he was looking in the wrong direction, and he did not know it.

God looks upon our heart. He knows where our heart is, what our heart is looking for. Are we hungry and really seeking fulness? Are we just content to be mediocre, halfway, never reaching the goal? God loves a seeker, and if we are seeking, even if we may seek in the wrong direction, sooner or later He will reveal Himself to us. That is the case with Saul.

SAUL MEETS THE LORD

The Bible tells us that one day he got the document from the chief priest to go to the foreign city of Damascus to seize upon those who believed in the Lord Jesus and were walking that way. He was to bring them to Jerusalem and sentence them to punishment, even unto death. Thank God for His longsuffering. The cord of love is long. He will let us go as far as we can, and then He will arrest us. Saul was on his way to Damascus, and when he was nearing that city at noontime, heaven opened, and a light from heaven shone upon him in such power he was smitten to the ground. Then he heard a voice in Hebrew: "Saul, Saul, why do you persecute Me? It is difficult for you to kick against the goads." It was not an angry voice. It was a sympathetic, loving, pitying, considering voice. "Saul, Saul, it is difficult. You are kicking against the goads. If you go on like this you will perish."

I believe we all know when the farmer plows the ground he puts an ox or a horse under a yoke, and then he will guide the yoke to till the ground. But sometimes that horse or that mule or that ox can be stubborn. It has its own way. It wants to go this way or that way. So when the animal does that, the farmer, who holds a goad, a sharp instrument in his other hand, will touch the leg of that animal. Of course he does not want to hurt it. He only wants to remind that animal that he has a master. You are here to do my will not your own will. It is only a slight touch, but how foolish, how stubborn that animal is! It will kick back, and when it kicks back, it hurts.

Brothers and sisters, don't you know that even before the foundation of the world God had already chosen you in Christ Jesus in love? Don't you know that even when you were in your mother's womb, He had already separated you for Himself? Don't you know that you are here with a purpose, not your purpose, but God's purpose? Don't you know that you are not free to do anything you like to do? You are His, created by Him for His purpose. You have a Master and you are here to do His will. If you do not, He will touch you with His goads softly, gently. But how you kick back, and you have to be touched again and again, until one day you realize it is useless; it is foolish. Brothers and sisters, it is foolish to live for yourself. You only hurt yourself, and our Lord will not like it. "Saul, Saul, why do you persecute Me?" He is not complaining that you persecute Him; He is thinking about you. Why? It is to your own hurt. Under that light his naked eye was blinded. Thank God for that! Sometimes our naked eyes are too open, too clear. As our Lord Jesus said, "If your eyes are blind, there is hope for you." When his naked eyes were blinded, his inner eyes were opened by God. He saw! He saw the righteous One. It pleased God to reveal His Son in him. What a revelation!

Saul considered our Lord Jesus as a man of Galilee, a carpenter, an impostor, someone to get rid of, who should not live on this earth. But now his inner eyes were opened, and he saw this Man whom he persecuted was none other than the Son of God. All the fulness of the Godhead dwells in Him bodily. He is the Heir of all things, the very Substance of the fulness of God, full of grace and truth, the righteous One, the risen One, the One in glory, the Master, irresistible, all-powerful.

He had a glimpse of the glory of the fulness of God in Christ Jesus. It was only a glimpse, but that glimpse changed his whole life. He began to realize all his past was wrong. He was heading in the wrong direction. He began to realize not only that our Lord Jesus is the Son of God, the Son of glory, the fulness of God, he also realized those humble believers that he seized upon, sentenced even to death, were living members of the body of Christ, part of that heavenly man. He had only a glimpse of it but that glimpse finished the old man, Saul, and brought in the new man Paul, the apostle. Paul means "little," not "asked for," but little, nothing.

SPIRITUAL FULNESS BEGINS WITH REVELATION

This is the beginning of the spiritual life of Paul. And do you know this is our beginning? The way to spiritual fulness begins with revelation. But the revelation we are talking about is not that which has already been revealed and been written in the Old Testament and New Testament because the revelation of God is completed in Christ Jesus. In former times God spoke through the prophets to our forefathers in pieces and in bits, but in the fulness of time He spoke to us in the Person of our Lord Jesus. So with the coming of the Lord Jesus, the revelations of God are completed. Nothing can be added; nothing can be taken away. We find that in Revelation 22. If you take away anything, the tree of life will be taken away from you. You cannot add anything to it; it is complete, it is fulfilled. So we are not talking about revelation in that sense. There is no more new revelation. Throughout the twentieth century many people proclaimed that they had new revelation and led people astray. No! There is no new revelation from above. You have revelation from below but not from above. We need to be careful about that. When you hear something that is contrary to the word of God already given, the faith once delivered to the saints, beware.

Yet we are talking about revelation, not in the objective sense, but in the subjective sense. That is to say, what God has already revealed and is written in the word of God, is objective. It is truth, forever true. It never changes; it is always working. No matter who you are or where you are, it works because it is truth; but it is objective. How can these objective truths become our subjective experience? It is through revelation. That is to say, the Holy Spirit will get hold of that which has already been revealed and bring it to us in such a living, personal way that it becomes an experience within us. That is revelation.

It is like the apostle Paul. On the way to Damascus he received a tremendous revelation.

The heavens opened, and light came from above. In that light he not only heard the voice but he saw the just One. That is revelation. And that revelation is so personal, so living, so operative, that what is revealed comes from heaven into your inner most being. It is not only there in heaven; it is here within you. You can say, "I heard it; I saw it; I knew it was true."

That is the revelation we are talking about. That is the beginning of our spiritual life. Think of yourself. How did you get saved? You may have been brought up in a Christian family. You may have heard the gospel so much that you could preach it. I did. I preached the gospel before I was saved. But God was distant to me. I prayed but my prayer hit the ceiling and came back to me. I did not know Him. I knew very much about Him, but I did not know Him, not until the Spirit of God convicted me of my sins. He convinced me that Jesus Christ is my Redeemer. If I confess my sins, He is faithful and righteous to forgive my sins and cleanse me from all my transgressions.

I still remember that afternoon in 1930 as I knelt before Him. He opened my understanding; I began to see that He is my Savior. I confessed to Him. He came into my heart. He is real. Revelation begins our spiritual life.

Brothers and sisters, do not tell me that you do not know revelation. If you do not, you are not even saved. No one can be saved without revelation. The natural man does not receive the things of God because they are folly to him. He does not know spiritual things because spiritual things can only be discerned spiritually. To the spiritually dead there is no way. They are completely shut out until one day God, in His mercy, looks upon your heart. He knows you are seeking. He reveals to you not only what you are, your sinfulness, He reveals to you the Savior, the Redeemer, the Lord. Every step of the way on the way to spiritual fulness begins with revelation. Remember this. When you first receive revelation you only get a glimpse of the fulness of God. He calls you by His glory, but the glory you see is just a little bit. If you obey the revelation given to you, more revelation will be given. You have a taste of the goodness of the

Lord, but that taste should increase your appetite, should make you hungry for more, just like that virgin in the Song of Solomon: "Kiss me with the kisses of your mouth, for your love is better than wine."

REVELATION CALLS FOR OBEDIENCE

He has kissed your neck, your stiff neck and made you soft, but don't stay there. Isn't that taste so sweet you want a closer, more intimate relationship with Him? Oh, I long for Him. Do you have a longing for Him? If you do, He will satisfy you. You are on the way to fulness. But remember, when revelation is given, it calls for obedience. If you do not obey the light, if you do not obey what He has revealed, that revelation will fade away. But if you obey, more will be given.

Remember Abraham. While he was in Ur of Chaldea, God called him. The God of glory appeared to him, and when the God of glory appeared to him, all the idols were broken. He could not stay in Ur of Chaldea. He heard a call: "Go out of thy land, and out of thy kindred, and come into the land which I will shew thee" (Acts

7:2). Abraham heard the voice; he saw the glory; he had to go. But unfortunately, he consulted with his father who had no vision of God. He obeyed halfway and got stuck in Haran. For many years there was no more revelation, no more glory, no more voice of God. But by the grace of God, God took Terah away and gave Abraham another chance. It was the same voice and the same command. There was nothing new. He only said, "Your father's house." Abraham obeyed.

What is the secret to spiritual fulness? On God's side it is revelation; on our side it is obedience. Obedience is better than sacrifice. Do we obey? Do we obey the light that He has given us? The apostle Paul testified: "I was not disobedient to the heavenly vision." That is the secret. Are we disobedient? Someone asked the question: "Why is it that Paul does not say, 'I was obedient to the heavenly vision' and yet he said, 'I was not disobedient to the heavenly vision.'" I think it tells us that naturally we are all disobedient. In our natural life we do not obey. We think it is folly. But thank God, he was not disobedient to the heavenly vision. So by the grace of God He made Paul obedient.

He testified that he did not consult with flesh and blood. Immediately he left for Arabia, and there for about three years, alone with God, he reread the Old Testament that he knew by heart. But it was under a new light; not by that dim light of the Law but by the bright light of Christ. He came back and announced that Jesus is *the* Christ. That is what is happening. If we have a seeking heart God will not fail to reveal His Son in you, and when He reveals, learn to obey.

DILIGENCE

There is another thing you can find in the life of Paul. The reason he seems to grow so fast into the fulness of God is because he is diligent. Even as Saul he was a diligent person; not only diligently seeking the Law, but diligently persecuting the Christians. He was not a lazy person. I think it was D. L. Moody who said, "Even Satan does not want a lazy man. He has no use for him."

We are all naturally lazy. We may be diligent in our own things, diligent in seeking the world, but when it comes to spiritual things we are lazy. It takes the grace of God, the exercise of our spirit, the working of the Holy Spirit in us to build up a new character in us, the character of Christ. Diligence!

Our Lord Jesus was the most diligent Person you could ever see on earth. In the book of Mark you will find the words "straightway, immediately." How diligent He was! And in the Bible, there is a lot of teaching on this Christian character of diligence.

In Hebrews 4:11—seeking diligently to enter into His rest.

Hebrews 11:6 says that God is a rewarder of those who seek Him diligently.

II Peter 1:5-11 says to diligently add virtue to faith. Add and add. Make your calling sure, election sure, that you may diligently enter into the kingdom of God.

The book of Proverbs is full of proverbs on diligence, on laziness.

God loves a diligent person. Do you really diligently seek Him? Do you really diligently read His word? Do you really diligently pray to Him? Do you really diligently serve Him? That is a Christian virtue that we need to cultivate. But of course we cannot make ourselves diligent by ourselves. It is the work of the Holy Spirit. He will remind us. Whenever He reminds us, obey.

THE SECRET TO SPIRITUAL FULNESS

What is the secret to spiritual fulness? Emptying—that is the secret. The measure of fulness is governed by the measure of emptying. The more we empty ourselves, the more we are filled with Christ. That is a spiritual law. Thank God, when we are saved the Spirit helps us to empty our sins by confessing and repenting. As we empty out our sins, redemption, forgiveness, salvation comes to us. He fills us with Himself. That is the beginning. Every time the Holy Spirit reminds us there is something in us that is not Christ, whether it is the world, whether it is sin, whether it is self, whether it is your flesh, whether it is from the enemy, learn to obey, cooperate. In the measure of your emptying will be the measure of your fulness. That is the reason why in your spiritual experience you find once you empty yourself you feel full, but that is your measure. But thank God, after awhile you begin to feel hungry again. Why? because He wants to fill you more. And that will go on and on and on until you come to your full capacity.

But our personal capacity is limited. That is why the church, the body of Christ is the fulness of Him who fills all and in all. We need the body. We need to have our inner man strengthened by the power of the Holy Spirit that Christ may dwell in our heart, reign in our heart, that we may apprehend with all the saints the length, the width, the depth, the height of the love of God, and to be filled with the fulness of God. We need one another.

Isn't it too wonderful, too glorious! How can it be? "Not by might, nor by power, but by the Spirit, says the Lord."

In Ephesians 3 we are told it is by His power that works in us above all that we can ask or think of, that we may be unto the glory of God.

And spiritual fulness is not for your glory, nor for my glory. It is for His glory.

Dear Lord, by Thy Spirit lead us into the truth of spiritual fulness that Thou mayest be glorified in the church in Christ Jesus. Amen.

QUESTION & ANSWER

Q: Would you address the matter of emptying a little more? You make it sound like it is so easy, as easy as pouring out a glass of water. I do not find it that simple to do. When the Holy Spirit convicts me of something, I struggle with it because these strongholds are so attached to me. They do not empty out so easily. Do you have a secret for everything?

A: This is a very good question, and I apologize if I gave the impression that emptying is so easy. I do not mean it. Probably because of the time, I could not explain it in detail. But remember one thing, spiritual principle is always simple. When you find a spiritual principle getting complicated, you know something is wrong. Spiritual principle is always simple, but simple does not mean easy. Spiritual experience is always complicated. So when you are talking about spiritual principle it has to be easy to understand. But when you get down into spiritual experience, it is quite complicated, and it is hard. So I think this is something we have to remember.

Emptying is the way to filling—very easy, very simple. If you want to be filled, you have to be emptied. What has to be emptied is *you*, and all the other things other than Christ in you. We do not know how full of ourselves we are. We do not really know how full we are of sins, of the world, of our flesh, of self, until the Holy Spirit begins to bring them to our attention. But God cannot do it all at once because we could not stand it. He knows our frame, so He has to do it little by little, piece by piece. And oftentimes you find in this emptying process it begins with things outside of you. Then it gets closer and closer until it touches the very self-life in you. So we have to remember that this emptying is a life-long process.

POURING OUT IS THE GRACE OF GOD

Thank God, when we first believed in the Lord Jesus, there was an emptying. It was the emptying of the sins that we were convicted with. Formerly, we felt that we were quite all right. But when the Holy Spirit begins to convict us, it brings us to the place where we feel that we are the vilest of sinners. We begin to hate sin, abhor it. We are afraid of it and want to get rid of it, but we cannot do it. No pouring can be done by yourself. No matter how strong your will, it is the grace of God. So just remember this. Every pouring is the grace of God. When you are convicted by the Holy Spirit, you know that you cannot do it, not even the simplest thing. It takes the grace of God, the love of the Lord Jesus to so constrain you, and He helps you to take it away. All you can do is to be willing. That is all you can do. You cannot do the pouring; He has to do it. So do not be so confident that you are able to pour out yourself. Impossible! You have to look to the Lord and He will do it.

THE PROCESS OF POURING OUT

Concerning this matter of pouring out, it is very complicated in the process. Every one of us is different. We do not go through spiritual experience in a uniform way. There is no such thing. God knows each one of us, so His dealing with us is special. To every one it is different. You cannot copy the other one. It is between you and the Lord, and that is the uniqueness of it. God deals with each one of us in an individual, personal way. It depends upon the wisdom and the knowledge of God because we do not know ourselves. We do not know how much that is not of Christ is within us. Therefore pouring depends upon the wisdom and the knowledge of God, and He will deal with each one of us individually, personally in the most effective way.

Some people may have a drastic dealing, a pouring out from the Lord from the very beginning, and after that the other pouring seems to be easier. But for some people the greatest battle is at the very last. He knows what is the best for you. So do not try to figure out what to pour out. If you try to do that you are in trouble. Self-analysis never helps. It is only in His light that we see light. So do not try to analyze yourself. I am fearful of what people are saying today, trying to dig deep into themselves to find what is there that needs to be gotten rid of. It is psychological; it is dangerous.

Dear brothers and sisters, so far as my own experience goes, I feel we should not analyze ourselves. All we can do is put ourselves in His hand and say, "Lord, I am here; I am willing." And He will do it.

THE PRINCIPLE OF CONSECRATION

But there are certain principles that probably will be helpful. I think this matter of pouring, whether it is easy or whether it is hard, depends basically upon your consecration. That is the reason why our Lord Jesus made this matter of consecration the first thing in Christian experience. After we have received all the mercies of God, what is our response? The first response is: "Present your bodies a living sacrifice." So in the experiences of the saints throughout the centuries you discover one thing. Those who have consecrated, who have given up themselves, given up their rights more absolutely, are those people that seem to make faster progress in spiritual life. So it is important in the very beginning when you are constrained by the love of Christ and you give yourself over to the Lord, the more absolute you are the better. Of course, that absoluteness is relative. In other words, as far as we know, that is all we can say. As far as you know, you lay everything at the feet of our Lord Jesus.

What does it mean? It does not mean that from now on you are qualified to work for Him. Not at all! This is a misunderstanding. It simply means that now you give the Lord the opportunity to pour you out and to fill in with Himself. That is consecration because God will never work against our will. He respects our will. He will not force us in any way. He will persuade us, convict us, even beseech us, beg us, but never force us. So that is the reason consecration is so important. And you will discover that at every pouring it deepens consecration. It enables you to let go of yourself a little bit more.

Oftentimes, when you find the Lord is demanding anything from you, you struggle. What is the struggling? It is like Jacob. You are struggling with the angel of the Lord because you do not want to let go of yourself. That is where the struggle is. But if you have a deeper consecration it makes it easier for the struggle to end. You will find that often the Lord will remind you: "Haven't you given yourself to Me? Haven't you promised that you are Mine? If you have, why do you struggle? Give in, let go, and let Me do what I want to bless you."

I believe that our consecration has a lot to do with this matter of pouring and filling. The deeper your consecration is, the greater will be the pouring, and the easier it will be. Maybe the struggling will be shortened, and thank God the filling will be more. So I think this is probably one of the principles in connection with pouring and filling. Again, I say this matter is very personal; only the Lord knows what you need.

When I first believed in the Lord Jesus, I think I loved the Lord, and I began to serve Him sincerely. But gradually the Lord began to touch me. I remember the first important thing that happened in my life was on this matter of baptism. I was baptized when I was a baby, but then a friend told me that did not count because I had no faith of my own. "Believe and be baptized."

I argued that I had been baptized in the name of the Father, the Son, and the Holy Spirit, and I could not do it a second time. Again and again God brought this matter to me. I searched the Scripture. I agreed that I needed to be baptized by immersion. That is the only baptism that counts. But I told the Lord I could not do it because I loved my father. My father was a Methodist pastor, and he loved the Lord. I did not want to hurt him, so I struggled over this matter. I would not let go.

One day my friend mentioned this to me again. I was angry. I knew but I could not. So he left me alone, and I was praying. I said, "Lord, You know. I will be baptized but not now. After I am independent, then I will do it." Suddenly the voice came to me: "He who loves his father and mother more than Me cannot be My disciple." That broke me; immediately I yielded.

I knocked at the door of Watchman Nee and when he asked me what I wanted, I said, "I want to be baptized."

He said, "Does your father know?"

And I said, "No, but I want to be baptized."

I was baptized the next day. And do you know that was the beginning of the opening up of light from above. In the past I was zealous for the Lord, but I was blind. I did it my own way, but from that time onward something was different. The light of the word of God began to open up. But that was not the end; that was the beginning. After one year I told my father. He was hurt, not because I was baptized by immersion, but because he felt I did not trust him. He said, "If you wanted to be baptized by immersion, I would have done it for you." And that hurt him.

So brothers and sisters, I feel so far as the principle of pouring is concerned, it is simple, but you cannot do it; I cannot do it; nobody can do it. And not only we cannot do it, we do not even know what to pour out. It is up to the Holy Spirit. It is only by His grace that we are able to do it. But He wants your cooperation. All He wants is that you be willing. I am willing to be willing to do Your will. That is all that is required.

So, I would encourage you that this matter of pouring is hard. We cannot let go ourselves; we cannot even let go of something that we have. But all these things, as Paul says, we must count as loss. Not only are they refuse, dirt, filth; they are hurtful. They are loss, not gain. And if by His grace we are willing to lose we will gain what is real gain, our Lord Jesus Christ. So may the Lord help us.

Other Books Printed By
Christian Testimony Ministry

SPEAKER	TITLE
DANA CONGDON	MARRIAGE, SINGLENESS, AND THE WILL OF GOD
	RECOVERY & RESTORATION
	THE HOLY SPIRIT
	HEBREWS
A.J. FLACK	TENT OF HIS SPLENDOUR
STEPHEN KAUNG	ACTS
	BE YE THEREFORE PERFECT
	CALLED OUT UNTO CHRIST
	CALLED TO THE FELLOWSHIP OF GOD'S SON
	DIVINE LIFE AND ORDER
	FOR ME TO LIVE IS CHRIST
	GLORIOUS LIBERTY OF THE CHILDREN OF GOD
	GOD'S PURPOSE FOR THE FAMILY
	I WILL BUILD MY CHURCH
	MEDITATIONS ON THE KINGDOM
	RECOVERY
	SPIRITUAL EXERCISE
	SPIRITUAL LIFE (II CORINTHIANS SERIES)
	TEACH US TO PRAY
	THE CROSS
	THE FULNESS OF CHRIST—IN THE BOOK OF REVELATION
	THE HEADSHIP OF CHRIST
	THE KINGDOM AND THE CHURCH
	THE KINGDOM OF GOD
	THE LAST CALL TO THE CHURCHES, THE CALL TO OVERCOME
	THE LIFE OF OUR LORD JESUS
	THE LIFE OF THE CHURCH, THE BODY OF CHRIST
	THE LORD'S TABLE
	TWO GUIDEPOSTS FOR INHERITING THE KINGDOM
	VISION OF CHRIST (REVELATION)
	WHO ARE WE?

WHY DO WE SO GATHER?
WORSHIP

LANCE LAMBERT

CALLED UNTO HIS ETERNAL GLORY
GOD'S ETERNAL PURPOSE
IN THE DAY OF THY POWER
JACOB I HAVE LOVED
LIVING FAITH
LESSONS FROM THE LIFE OF MOSES
LOVE DIVINE
MY HOUSE SHALL BE A HOUSE OF PRAYER
PREPARATION FOR THE COMING OF THE LORD
REIGNING WITH CHRIST
SPIRITUAL CHARACTER
THE GOSPEL OF THE KINGDOM
THE IMPORTANCE OF COVERING
THE LAST DAYS AND GOD'S PRIORITIES
THE PRIZE
THE SUPREMACY OF JESUS CHRIST
THINE IS THE POWER!
THOU ART MINE

T. AUSTIN-SPARKS

THE LORD'S TESTIMONY AND THE WORLD NEED

HARVEY CEDARS CONFERENCE

STEPHEN KAUNG

HEAVENLY VISION
SPIRITUAL RESPONSIBILITY

CONGDON, HILE, KAUNG

SPIRITUAL MINISTRY
SPIRITUAL AUTHORITY
SPIRITUAL HOUSE
SPIRITUAL SUBMISSION

STEPHEN KAUNG

SPIRITUAL KNOWLEDGE
SPIRITUAL POWER
SPIRITUAL REALITY
SPIRITUAL VALUE
SPIRITUAL BLESSING
SPIRITUAL DISCERNMENT

www.ingramcontent.com/pod-product-compliance
Lightning Source LLC
Chambersburg PA
CBHW060712030426
42337CB00017B/2840